MEAL PREP MEAL PLANNER

MEAL PREP

MEAL PLANNER

YOUR ORGANIZER TO PLAN WEEKLY MENUS, SHOPPING LISTS, AND MEALS

LISA DANIELSON

ROCKRIDGE
PRESS

Interior and Cover Designer: Karmen Lizzul
Art Producer: Karen Williams
Editor: Pam Kingsley
Production Editor: Mia Moran
Author photo courtesy of © Maggie Yahvah

ISBN: Print 978-1-64739-374-8
R0

CONTENTS

INTRODUCTION

With my busy life, my goal is to minimize my time in the kitchen so that I can maximize quality time with my family, and I am here to show you how to do the same.

I am a nutrition specialist, and a motto I share with my clients is "Work smarter, not harder"—that is where meal prep comes in. Let's face it, our days are packed—work, car pool, chores, appointments—but we still need to put food on the table every day. This is where planning and preparing your food in advance can help you make the most of your time *and* your paycheck.

This planner will fast-track you from a beginner to a pro meal prepper in no time. Organization is the first step to starting anything new, especially when it comes to planning, shopping, preparing, and storing your meals in the easiest way possible. I've designed this planner to be your new best friend so each week you will know what to shop for, the ingredients to prep ahead, and which meals to freeze so you can reheat them on your busiest nights.

Let's get started!

MEAL PREP 101

MEAL PREP REFERS TO the
planning, shopping, preparation, and storage of
food for the week (or even further) ahead. Meal
prep will save you time, energy, and money as you
eliminate last-minute mad dashes to the supermarket to pick up something—anything—to feed
your family dinner that night. Once you find your
meal prep groove, you'll be shopping, cooking, and
banking meals all in the same day, leaving you
more time during the week to be with your family
instead of rushing around. You'll also find that you
and your family will eat healthier, a result of por-
tion control and eliminating impulse buying from
your shopping trips. Home-cooked, nutritious
meals ready when you are—what could be better?

Now, let's dig into the strategies that will turn
you into a meal prep planner!

KEEP IT SIMPLE

One of the most common mistakes in meal prep is overdoing it—planning three different meals for every day of the week. That equates to very long (and multiple) meal prep days; it also triples the amount of food you need to buy.

The secret is to streamline planning and learn to love leftovers. Make enough for dinner on Monday and then enjoy it again on Thursday or for lunch on Tuesday and Friday, and then freeze whatever might still be left for a future grab-and-go meal.

The same goes for breakfast; use your slow cooker or pressure cooker to make a big batch on Sunday, and then divide it up into individual portions for each morning. An easy way to change it up is to add different mix-ins like nuts, fruit, maple syrup, brown sugar, or cinnamon.

Repeat meals will simplify your prep and your shopping list.

BATCH PREP

Whether it's roasting a big pan of broccoli or making a slow cooker full of taco soup, batch cooking is the cornerstone of meal prep. The goal is to cut down on cooking time the day you intend to eat a meal, which you can do by preparing an entire meal ahead of time or precooking elements of it, like browning several pounds of ground beef to have on hand to make a shortcut chili or add to a casserole. Grains are also great to cook in advance. The goal is to cook once and eat twice (or three or four times). If you have leftovers...freeze them! There is nothing quite like coming home after a busy day to a meal that just needs warming up!

BANKING MEALS

When making a big batch meal like a soup, stew, or casserole, be sure to put one or two servings in individual containers to freeze for lunch at a later date. These "emergency stashes" are lifesavers on busy days when you need a meal fast. For the rest, either cover and refrigerate to enjoy as your family's meal later in the week or transfer it to an airtight container or zip-top plastic bag to freeze for future use.

Any time you have leftovers from a meal, divide them into individual portions and add them to your bank of ready-to-go freezer meals.

STORAGE

Proper food storage is key to meal prep, whether in the refrigerator or freezer. Use high-quality containers, package your food correctly, and be sure to label and date everything so you don't lose track of what you have stored. Your prepped meals are precious cargo, and you don't want to lose anything to spoilage or freezer burn!

CONTAINERS

Whether they are for use in the refrigerator or freezer, containers should be airtight and dishwasher-safe. For single-serving portions, purchase containers that are microwave-safe; that way they can do double duty for storage and serving.

Whether you use glass or plastic is your choice, but keep in mind that glass containers weigh more and don't stack as tightly as plastic containers of the same size. If you intend to use glass containers in the freezer, be sure they are labeled freezer-safe or are made of tempered glass, like canning jars. But even then you need to be careful to leave plenty of headspace inside each glass container, because the food will expand as it freezes; the glass can burst if there's not enough room.

Invest in several sizes of containers. To store a meal (like a stew or soup) for four or more, 6- to 8-cup containers work well; for individual servings, 2-cup containers are better. You may also want to get containers in different shapes that are better suited to storing salads or sandwiches. Multi-compartment containers are a favorite of mine for carrying a combination of lunch and snacks to work.

If you are fond of salads, 34-ounce mason jars are a great way to store them. I also like having 2-ounce containers on hand to use for dressing or any crunchy toppings that I want to keep separate from my salad until I'm ready to eat.

PLASTIC STORAGE BAGS

In addition to containers, you'll want to have zip-top plastic bags on hand in large and small sizes. I use the quart and gallon bags most frequently. If you'll be using them in the freezer, buy heavy-duty freezer bags, which will protect against freezer burn. For the best storage results, be sure to press out as much air as you can when sealing the bag. And if you're freezing, lay the bag flat on a baking sheet so the food is in an even layer; then transfer to the freezer. Remove the baking sheet once the food is frozen; doing this will allow you to stack the bags on top of one another, taking up way less precious freezer space.

LABELING

Whether you are storing in containers or plastic bags, be sure to properly label them with the following:

- The name of the meal
- The date it was prepared/frozen
- If it is a pre-prepped ingredient (like browned meat or chopped onions), the amount that is in the container, like 1 pound or 1 cup

I like to use dissolvable labels; these just melt away when you put the container in the dishwasher. You can find them online.

REHEATING

Here are some general guidelines:

FROM THE FRIDGE

- Most meals can be reheated in the microwave; start at 50 percent power in 1- to 2-minute increments until the food is warmed through. Make sure to keep the food covered with a paper towel or the container lid (set loosely on top) to avoid splatter.
- Only reheat food once to avoid the growth of unwanted bacteria. That means you should only reheat what you will eat in one sitting.

FROM THE FREEZER

- Food such as grains, fruits, and vegetables can be reheated straight from the freezer. I start at 50 percent power for 1 to 2 minutes and then test to see how much warmer it needs to be. After that you can use shorter bursts (30 seconds) on full power to heat these foods thoroughly.

- Most other food needs to be moved to the fridge to thaw before heating, which takes 12 to 24 hours. Get in the habit of making this switch the night before so your food will be ready for reheating for lunch or dinner.
- Do not thaw food at room temperature, only in the refrigerator. Otherwise, you risk the possibility of a foodborne illness like E. coli or salmonella.

HOW TO USE THIS MEAL PLANNER

This meal planner is designed to take the guesswork out of meal prep. Not only will you know what you will be eating for every meal of every day in the coming week, but you will also go to the store knowing exactly what you need to buy. Being organized is more than half the battle! Each week of the planner is designed so you can write down what meals you will be having that week (even snacks), your grocery list, when you will do your meal prep, and what you will be prepping. It will also help you keep track of the meals you already have prepped that are ready and waiting in your fridge or freezer. It doesn't get much easier than that!

BREAKFAST, LUNCH/SNACK, AND DINNER

Your Weekly Meal Planners give you plenty of space to list what you'll be having for breakfast, lunch (and snack), and dinner Saturday through Friday.

Here are some quick tips to make it as easy as possible:

- Review your calendar for the week. What nights will you be too busy to cook? That's when you want fully prepped meals in the fridge, whether you prep them that week or lean into your frozen stash. (Just remember to put frozen food in the fridge the night before to thaw.)
- Take a look at what you still have on hand, particularly any perishables that might be near the end of their life spans so you can work them into your menu to eliminate waste.
- Decide what you need to make ahead of time for the meals you will be having that week.

→ Think about what ready-to-eat items from the supermarket would work well in your menu to save additional time. It could be fresh pico de gallo from the deli or heat-and-serve rice.

WEEK'S MEAL PREP

This is where you will list what advance meal prep you will be doing for the week and when you will do it. I suggest doing the bulk of it on the weekend if that syncs with your schedule. I find Saturday to be a great time to take inventory of my ingredients and to think about how I can use what I still have in that week's menu. Once I've done my inventory and settled on my menu, I shop for what I need.

Sunday is my primary meal prep day, when I batch cook full meals and precook ingredients. Sometimes around midweek I might do additional prep to finish out the week. All of these tasks should be noted in the Week's Meal Prep section of the planner.

MEAL TRACKER

As you start to meal prep, you'll want to keep track of what you have banked. Your Meal Tracker is where you will do that. Write down the meals and prepped ingredients you already have stashed in your fridge or freezer. As you use them, cross them off so you always have an accurate accounting of what is available to you when planning the week's meals. That also means tracking single servings of leftovers that you store in the freezer.

SHOPPING LIST

This can be the trickiest part for some people: getting their Shopping List just right. Only include what you need to pick up at the store to make the meals you have chosen for that week. If chili is on the menu, check that you have the right spices and canned goods in the pantry. Note anything you're missing or low on, as well as the perishable ingredients you'll need to finish the recipe. Most of us have a running tally in our heads of what items we have on hand, but if you make a habit of checking your inventory, you won't ever be caught short. This also includes the items you use regularly to prep your breakfast and lunch/snack.

WEEK: April 4—April 11

SAT	B	Avocado toast
	L/S	Frozen store-bought cheese pizza, beef jerky
	D	Corn chowder
SUN	B	Chia pudding
	L/S	Veggie sandwich, protein bar
	D	Coconut curry
MON	B	Oatmeal with berries
	L/S	Turkey panini, protein bar
	D	Veggie stir-fry
TUE	B	Chia pudding
	L/S	Taco salad, apple with peanut butter
	D	Corn chowder
WED	B	Oatmeal with berries
	L/S	Taco salad, beef jerky
	D	Coconut curry
THU	B	Avocado toast
	L/S	Turkey wrap, protein bar
	D	Veggie stir-fry
FRI	B	Oatmeal with berries
	L/S	Veggie sandwich, apple with peanut butter
	D	Steak tacos

WEEK'S MEAL PREP

On Saturday:

Rinse lettuce, pull apart into leaves

Make chia pudding

Make double batch corn chowder

Put frozen coconut curry in fridge to thaw

On Sunday:

Slice tomatoes

Grill steak for tacos

Start big batch of overnight oatmeal

MEAL TRACKER

Cooked brown rice (in fridge)

Chopped onions (in freezer)

Seasoned taco meat (in freezer)

Coconut curry (in freezer)

SHOPPING LIST

1 container strawberries

2 apples

2 avocados

1 head butter lettuce

2 Roma tomatoes

1 lb skirt steak

1 large container Greek yogurt

1 package sliced Colby-Jack cheese

1/2 lb sliced turkey breast

1 container hummus

1 bag frozen sliced peppers and onions

1 bag frozen corn

1 bag frozen stir-fry vegetables

1 bag frozen shelled edamame

1 frozen personal cheese pizza

2 taco salad shells

1 package beef jerky

3 protein bars

WEEKLY MEAL PLANNERS

WEEK:

SAT	B	
	L / S	
	D	
SUN	B	
	L / S	
	D	
MON	B	
	L / S	
	D	
TUE	B	
	L / S	
	D	
WED	B	
	L / S	
	D	
THU	B	
	L / S	
	D	
FRI	B	
	L / S	
	D	

WEEK'S MEAL PREP

SHOPPING LIST

MEAL TRACKER

WEEK:

SAT	B	
	L/S	
	D	
SUN	B	
	L/S	
	D	
MON	B	
	L/S	
	D	
TUE	B	
	L/S	
	D	
WED	B	
	L/S	
	D	
THU	B	
	L/S	
	D	
FRI	B	
	L/S	
	D	

WEEK'S MEAL PREP

SHOPPING LIST

MEAL TRACKER

WEEK:

SAT	B	
	L/S	
	D	
SUN	B	
	L/S	
	D	
MON	B	
	L/S	
	D	
TUE	B	
	L/S	
	D	
WED	B	
	L/S	
	D	
THU	B	
	L/S	
	D	
FRI	B	
	L/S	
	D	

WEEK'S MEAL PREP

SHOPPING LIST

MEAL TRACKER

WEEK:

SAT	B	
	L / S	
	D	
SUN	B	
	L / S	
	D	
MON	B	
	L / S	
	D	
TUE	B	
	L / S	
	D	
WED	B	
	L / S	
	D	
THU	B	
	L / S	
	D	
FRI	B	
	L / S	
	D	

WEEK'S MEAL PREP

SHOPPING LIST

MEAL TRACKER

WEEK:

SAT	B	
	L / S	
	D	
SUN	B	
	L / S	
	D	
MON	B	
	L / S	
	D	
TUE	B	
	L / S	
	D	
WED	B	
	L / S	
	D	
THU	B	
	L / S	
	D	
FRI	B	
	L / S	
	D	

WEEK'S MEAL PREP

SHOPPING LIST

MEAL TRACKER

WEEK:

SAT	B	
	L/S	
	D	
SUN	B	
	L/S	
	D	
MON	B	
	L/S	
	D	
TUE	B	
	L/S	
	D	
WED	B	
	L/S	
	D	
THU	B	
	L/S	
	D	
FRI	B	
	L/S	
	D	

WEEK'S MEAL PREP

SHOPPING LIST

MEAL TRACKER

WEEK:

SAT	B	
	L / S	
	D	
SUN	B	
	L / S	
	D	
MON	B	
	L / S	
	D	
TUE	B	
	L / S	
	D	
WED	B	
	L / S	
	D	
THU	B	
	L / S	
	D	
FRI	B	
	L / S	
	D	

WEEK'S MEAL PREP

SHOPPING LIST

MEAL TRACKER

WEEK:

SAT	B	
	L / S	
	D	
SUN	B	
	L / S	
	D	
MON	B	
	L / S	
	D	
TUE	B	
	L / S	
	D	
WED	B	
	L / S	
	D	
THU	B	
	L / S	
	D	
FRI	B	
	L / S	
	D	

WEEK'S MEAL PREP

SHOPPING LIST

MEAL TRACKER

WEEK:

SAT	B	
	L/S	
	D	
SUN	B	
	L/S	
	D	
MON	B	
	L/S	
	D	
TUE	B	
	L/S	
	D	
WED	B	
	L/S	
	D	
THU	B	
	L/S	
	D	
FRI	B	
	L/S	
	D	

WEEK'S MEAL PREP

SHOPPING LIST

MEAL TRACKER

WEEK:

SAT	B	
	L/S	
	D	
SUN	B	
	L/S	
	D	
MON	B	
	L/S	
	D	
TUE	B	
	L/S	
	D	
WED	B	
	L/S	
	D	
THU	B	
	L/S	
	D	
FRI	B	
	L/S	
	D	

WEEK'S MEAL PREP

SHOPPING LIST

MEAL TRACKER

WEEK:

SAT	B	
	L / S	
	D	
SUN	B	
	L / S	
	D	
MON	B	
	L / S	
	D	
TUE	B	
	L / S	
	D	
WED	B	
	L / S	
	D	
THU	B	
	L / S	
	D	
FRI	B	
	L / S	
	D	

WEEK'S MEAL PREP

SHOPPING LIST

MEAL TRACKER

WEEK:

SAT	B	
	L/S	
	D	
SUN	B	
	L/S	
	D	
MON	B	
	L/S	
	D	
TUE	B	
	L/S	
	D	
WED	B	
	L/S	
	D	
THU	B	
	L/S	
	D	
FRI	B	
	L/S	
	D	

WEEK'S MEAL PREP

SHOPPING LIST

MEAL TRACKER

WEEK:

SAT	B	
	L/S	
	D	
SUN	B	
	L/S	
	D	
MON	B	
	L/S	
	D	
TUE	B	
	L/S	
	D	
WED	B	
	L/S	
	D	
THU	B	
	L/S	
	D	
FRI	B	
	L/S	
	D	

WEEK'S MEAL PREP

SHOPPING LIST

MEAL TRACKER

WEEK:

SAT	B	
	L / S	
	D	
SUN	B	
	L / S	
	D	
MON	B	
	L / S	
	D	
TUE	B	
	L / S	
	D	
WED	B	
	L / S	
	D	
THU	B	
	L / S	
	D	
FRI	B	
	L / S	
	D	

WEEK'S MEAL PREP

SHOPPING LIST

MEAL TRACKER

WEEK:

SAT	B	
	L / S	
	D	
SUN	B	
	L / S	
	D	
MON	B	
	L / S	
	D	
TUE	B	
	L / S	
	D	
WED	B	
	L / S	
	D	
THU	B	
	L / S	
	D	
FRI	B	
	L / S	
	D	

WEEK'S MEAL PREP

SHOPPING LIST

MEAL TRACKER

WEEK:

SAT	B	
	L / S	
	D	
SUN	B	
	L / S	
	D	
MON	B	
	L / S	
	D	
TUE	B	
	L / S	
	D	
WED	B	
	L / S	
	D	
THU	B	
	L / S	
	D	
FRI	B	
	L / S	
	D	

WEEK'S MEAL PREP

SHOPPING LIST

MEAL TRACKER

WEEK:

SAT	B	
	L / S	
	D	
SUN	B	
	L / S	
	D	
MON	B	
	L / S	
	D	
TUE	B	
	L / S	
	D	
WED	B	
	L / S	
	D	
THU	B	
	L / S	
	D	
FRI	B	
	L / S	
	D	

WEEK'S MEAL PREP

SHOPPING LIST

MEAL TRACKER

WEEK:

SAT	B	
	L/S	
	D	
SUN	B	
	L/S	
	D	
MON	B	
	L/S	
	D	
TUE	B	
	L/S	
	D	
WED	B	
	L/S	
	D	
THU	B	
	L/S	
	D	
FRI	B	
	L/S	
	D	

WEEK'S MEAL PREP

SHOPPING LIST

MEAL TRACKER

WEEK:

SAT	B	
	L / S	
	D	
SUN	B	
	L / S	
	D	
MON	B	
	L / S	
	D	
TUE	B	
	L / S	
	D	
WED	B	
	L / S	
	D	
THU	B	
	L / S	
	D	
FRI	B	
	L / S	
	D	

WEEK'S MEAL PREP

SHOPPING LIST

MEAL TRACKER

WEEK:

SAT	B	
	L / S	
	D	
SUN	B	
	L / S	
	D	
MON	B	
	L / S	
	D	
TUE	B	
	L / S	
	D	
WED	B	
	L / S	
	D	
THU	B	
	L / S	
	D	
FRI	B	
	L / S	
	D	

WEEK'S MEAL PREP

SHOPPING LIST

MEAL TRACKER

WEEK:

SAT	B	
	L/S	
	D	
SUN	B	
	L/S	
	D	
MON	B	
	L/S	
	D	
TUE	B	
	L/S	
	D	
WED	B	
	L/S	
	D	
THU	B	
	L/S	
	D	
FRI	B	
	L/S	
	D	

WEEK'S MEAL PREP

SHOPPING LIST

MEAL TRACKER

WEEK:

SAT	B	
	L / S	
	D	
SUN	B	
	L / S	
	D	
MON	B	
	L / S	
	D	
TUE	B	
	L / S	
	D	
WED	B	
	L / S	
	D	
THU	B	
	L / S	
	D	
FRI	B	
	L / S	
	D	

WEEK'S MEAL PREP

SHOPPING LIST

MEAL TRACKER

WEEK:

SAT	B	
	L / S	
	D	
SUN	B	
	L / S	
	D	
MON	B	
	L / S	
	D	
TUE	B	
	L / S	
	D	
WED	B	
	L / S	
	D	
THU	B	
	L / S	
	D	
FRI	B	
	L / S	
	D	

WEEK'S MEAL PREP

SHOPPING LIST

MEAL TRACKER

WEEK:

SAT	B	
	L / S	
	D	
SUN	B	
	L / S	
	D	
MON	B	
	L / S	
	D	
TUE	B	
	L / S	
	D	
WED	B	
	L / S	
	D	
THU	B	
	L / S	
	D	
FRI	B	
	L / S	
	D	

WEEK'S MEAL PREP

SHOPPING LIST

MEAL TRACKER

WEEK:

SAT	B	
	L/S	
	D	
SUN	B	
	L/S	
	D	
MON	B	
	L/S	
	D	
TUE	B	
	L/S	
	D	
WED	B	
	L/S	
	D	
THU	B	
	L/S	
	D	
FRI	B	
	L/S	
	D	

WEEK'S MEAL PREP

SHOPPING LIST

MEAL TRACKER

WEEK:

SAT	B	
	L / S	
	D	
SUN	B	
	L / S	
	D	
MON	B	
	L / S	
	D	
TUE	B	
	L / S	
	D	
WED	B	
	L / S	
	D	
THU	B	
	L / S	
	D	
FRI	B	
	L / S	
	D	

WEEK'S MEAL PREP

SHOPPING LIST

MEAL TRACKER

WEEK:

SAT	B	
	L / S	
	D	
SUN	B	
	L / S	
	D	
MON	B	
	L / S	
	D	
TUE	B	
	L / S	
	D	
WED	B	
	L / S	
	D	
THU	B	
	L / S	
	D	
FRI	B	
	L / S	
	D	

WEEK'S MEAL PREP

SHOPPING LIST

MEAL TRACKER

WEEK:

SAT	B	
	L / S	
	D	
SUN	B	
	L / S	
	D	
MON	B	
	L / S	
	D	
TUE	B	
	L / S	
	D	
WED	B	
	L / S	
	D	
THU	B	
	L / S	
	D	
FRI	B	
	L / S	
	D	

WEEK'S MEAL PREP

SHOPPING LIST

MEAL TRACKER

WEEK:

SAT	B	
	L / S	
	D	
SUN	B	
	L / S	
	D	
MON	B	
	L / S	
	D	
TUE	B	
	L / S	
	D	
WED	B	
	L / S	
	D	
THU	B	
	L / S	
	D	
FRI	B	
	L / S	
	D	

WEEK'S MEAL PREP

SHOPPING LIST

MEAL TRACKER

WEEK:

SAT	B	
	L/S	
	D	
SUN	B	
	L/S	
	D	
MON	B	
	L/S	
	D	
TUE	B	
	L/S	
	D	
WED	B	
	L/S	
	D	
THU	B	
	L/S	
	D	
FRI	B	
	L/S	
	D	

WEEK'S MEAL PREP

SHOPPING LIST

MEAL TRACKER

WEEK:

SAT	B	
	L / S	
	D	
SUN	B	
	L / S	
	D	
MON	B	
	L / S	
	D	
TUE	B	
	L / S	
	D	
WED	B	
	L / S	
	D	
THU	B	
	L / S	
	D	
FRI	B	
	L / S	
	D	

WEEK'S MEAL PREP

SHOPPING LIST

MEAL TRACKER

WEEK:

SAT	B	
	L/S	
	D	
SUN	B	
	L/S	
	D	
MON	B	
	L/S	
	D	
TUE	B	
	L/S	
	D	
WED	B	
	L/S	
	D	
THU	B	
	L/S	
	D	
FRI	B	
	L/S	
	D	

WEEK'S MEAL PREP

SHOPPING LIST

MEAL TRACKER

WEEK:

SAT	B	
	L/S	
	D	
SUN	B	
	L/S	
	D	
MON	B	
	L/S	
	D	
TUE	B	
	L/S	
	D	
WED	B	
	L/S	
	D	
THU	B	
	L/S	
	D	
FRI	B	
	L/S	
	D	

WEEK'S MEAL PREP

SHOPPING LIST

MEAL TRACKER

WEEK:

SAT	B	
	L / S	
	D	
SUN	B	
	L / S	
	D	
MON	B	
	L / S	
	D	
TUE	B	
	L / S	
	D	
WED	B	
	L / S	
	D	
THU	B	
	L / S	
	D	
FRI	B	
	L / S	
	D	

WEEK'S MEAL PREP

SHOPPING LIST

MEAL TRACKER

WEEK:

SAT	B	
	L / S	
	D	
SUN	B	
	L / S	
	D	
MON	B	
	L / S	
	D	
TUE	B	
	L / S	
	D	
WED	B	
	L / S	
	D	
THU	B	
	L / S	
	D	
FRI	B	
	L / S	
	D	

WEEK'S MEAL PREP

SHOPPING LIST

MEAL TRACKER

WEEK:

SAT	B	
	L / S	
	D	
SUN	B	
	L / S	
	D	
MON	B	
	L / S	
	D	
TUE	B	
	L / S	
	D	
WED	B	
	L / S	
	D	
THU	B	
	L / S	
	D	
FRI	B	
	L / S	
	D	

WEEK'S MEAL PREP

SHOPPING LIST

MEAL TRACKER

WEEK:

SAT	B	
	L / S	
	D	
SUN	B	
	L / S	
	D	
MON	B	
	L / S	
	D	
TUE	B	
	L / S	
	D	
WED	B	
	L / S	
	D	
THU	B	
	L / S	
	D	
FRI	B	
	L / S	
	D	

WEEK'S MEAL PREP

SHOPPING LIST

MEAL TRACKER

WEEK:

SAT	B	
	L / S	
	D	
SUN	B	
	L / S	
	D	
MON	B	
	L / S	
	D	
TUE	B	
	L / S	
	D	
WED	B	
	L / S	
	D	
THU	B	
	L / S	
	D	
FRI	B	
	L / S	
	D	

WEEK'S MEAL PREP

SHOPPING LIST

MEAL TRACKER

WEEK:

SAT	B	
	L / S	
	D	
SUN	B	
	L / S	
	D	
MON	B	
	L / S	
	D	
TUE	B	
	L / S	
	D	
WED	B	
	L / S	
	D	
THU	B	
	L / S	
	D	
FRI	B	
	L / S	
	D	

WEEK'S MEAL PREP

SHOPPING LIST

MEAL TRACKER

WEEK:

SAT	B	
	L/S	
	D	
SUN	B	
	L/S	
	D	
MON	B	
	L/S	
	D	
TUE	B	
	L/S	
	D	
WED	B	
	L/S	
	D	
THU	B	
	L/S	
	D	
FRI	B	
	L/S	
	D	

WEEK'S MEAL PREP

_____

_____

_____

_____

_____

_____

_____

SHOPPING LIST

MEAL TRACKER

_____

_____

_____

_____

_____

_____

_____

WEEK:

SAT	B	
	L / S	
	D	
SUN	B	
	L / S	
	D	
MON	B	
	L / S	
	D	
TUE	B	
	L / S	
	D	
WED	B	
	L / S	
	D	
THU	B	
	L / S	
	D	
FRI	B	
	L / S	
	D	

WEEK'S MEAL PREP

SHOPPING LIST

MEAL TRACKER

WEEK:

SAT	B	
	L / S	
	D	
SUN	B	
	L / S	
	D	
MON	B	
	L / S	
	D	
TUE	B	
	L / S	
	D	
WED	B	
	L / S	
	D	
THU	B	
	L / S	
	D	
FRI	B	
	L / S	
	D	

WEEK'S MEAL PREP

SHOPPING LIST

MEAL TRACKER

WEEK:

SAT	B	
	L / S	
	D	
SUN	B	
	L / S	
	D	
MON	B	
	L / S	
	D	
TUE	B	
	L / S	
	D	
WED	B	
	L / S	
	D	
THU	B	
	L / S	
	D	
FRI	B	
	L / S	
	D	

WEEK'S MEAL PREP

SHOPPING LIST

MEAL TRACKER

WEEK:

SAT	B	
	L/S	
	D	
SUN	B	
	L/S	
	D	
MON	B	
	L/S	
	D	
TUE	B	
	L/S	
	D	
WED	B	
	L/S	
	D	
THU	B	
	L/S	
	D	
FRI	B	
	L/S	
	D	

WEEK'S MEAL PREP

SHOPPING LIST

MEAL TRACKER

WEEK:

SAT	B	
	L / S	
	D	
SUN	B	
	L / S	
	D	
MON	B	
	L / S	
	D	
TUE	B	
	L / S	
	D	
WED	B	
	L / S	
	D	
THU	B	
	L / S	
	D	
FRI	B	
	L / S	
	D	

WEEK'S MEAL PREP

SHOPPING LIST

MEAL TRACKER

WEEK:

SAT	B	
	L/S	
	D	
SUN	B	
	L/S	
	D	
MON	B	
	L/S	
	D	
TUE	B	
	L/S	
	D	
WED	B	
	L/S	
	D	
THU	B	
	L/S	
	D	
FRI	B	
	L/S	
	D	

WEEK'S MEAL PREP

SHOPPING LIST

MEAL TRACKER

WEEK:

SAT	B	
	L / S	
	D	
SUN	B	
	L / S	
	D	
MON	B	
	L / S	
	D	
TUE	B	
	L / S	
	D	
WED	B	
	L / S	
	D	
THU	B	
	L / S	
	D	
FRI	B	
	L / S	
	D	

WEEK'S MEAL PREP

SHOPPING LIST

MEAL TRACKER

WEEK:

SAT	B	
	L/S	
	D	
SUN	B	
	L/S	
	D	
MON	B	
	L/S	
	D	
TUE	B	
	L/S	
	D	
WED	B	
	L/S	
	D	
THU	B	
	L/S	
	D	
FRI	B	
	L/S	
	D	

WEEK'S MEAL PREP

SHOPPING LIST

MEAL TRACKER

WEEK:

SAT	B	
	L/S	
	D	
SUN	B	
	L/S	
	D	
MON	B	
	L/S	
	D	
TUE	B	
	L/S	
	D	
WED	B	
	L/S	
	D	
THU	B	
	L/S	
	D	
FRI	B	
	L/S	
	D	

WEEK'S MEAL PREP

SHOPPING LIST

MEAL TRACKER

WEEK:

SAT	B	
	L/S	
	D	
SUN	B	
	L/S	
	D	
MON	B	
	L/S	
	D	
TUE	B	
	L/S	
	D	
WED	B	
	L/S	
	D	
THU	B	
	L/S	
	D	
FRI	B	
	L/S	
	D	

WEEK'S MEAL PREP

SHOPPING LIST

MEAL TRACKER

WEEK:

SAT	B	
	L / S	
	D	
SUN	B	
	L / S	
	D	
MON	B	
	L / S	
	D	
TUE	B	
	L / S	
	D	
WED	B	
	L / S	
	D	
THU	B	
	L / S	
	D	
FRI	B	
	L / S	
	D	

WEEK'S MEAL PREP

SHOPPING LIST

MEAL TRACKER

WEEK:

SAT	B	
	L/S	
	D	
SUN	B	
	L/S	
	D	
MON	B	
	L/S	
	D	
TUE	B	
	L/S	
	D	
WED	B	
	L/S	
	D	
THU	B	
	L/S	
	D	
FRI	B	
	L/S	
	D	

WEEK'S MEAL PREP

SHOPPING LIST

MEAL TRACKER

ABOUT THE AUTHOR

 **Lisa Danielson**, aka "Veggie Lisa," has a deep-rooted love for all things green and a passion for helping other plant-based eaters create healthy menus that fit into their busy lifestyles. She currently runs an online personal training and nutrition program, teaches aerobics, and is a National Physique Committee fitness competitor. Lisa is the author of three vegetarian cookbooks and a mom to four kiddos, ages 6 to 16, and her mini goldendoodle, Duke. Lisa's motto is "Living a healthy lifestyle doesn't have to be complicated."

CPSIA information can be obtained
at www.ICGtesting.com
Printed in the USA
JSHW051054280820
7534JS00005B/13